Meditations, With Distractions

Also by James J. McAuley

Verse Collections
Coming & Going, 1989
Recital, 1982
After the Blizzard, 1975
Draft Balance Sheet, 1970
A New Address, 1965
Observations, 1960

Chapbooks
The Gingriad, 1995
The Exile's Book of Hours, 1982
The Exile's Recurring Nightmare, 1974
Home & Away, 1974

Verse Satire
The Revolution
    Lantern Theatre, Dublin, 1966

Libretto
Praise!
    Composer, Wendal Jones
    Spokane Opera House, 1981

Meditations, With Distractions

Poems, 1988–98

James J. McAuley

The University of Arkansas Press
Fayetteville
2000

05 04 03 02 01   5 4 3 2 1

Designer: John Coghlan

⊖ The paper used in this publication meets the minimum requirements
of the American National Standard for Permanence of Paper for Printed
Library Materials Z39.48–1984.

Library of Congress Cataloging-in-Publication Data
McAuley, James J.
    Meditations, with distractions : poems, 1988-98 / James J. McAuley.
        p.   cm.
      ISBN 1-55728-700-7
    I. Title.
      PR6025.A1612 M43 2001
        821'.914–dc21

                                                        00-011645

for Deirdre

Acknowledgments

The author would like to thank the editors of the following publications for permission to include the following poems, versions of which they published:

"Holyhead," "A Farewell to His Poems," *In Cognito;*
"Waiting Room," "After a Chorus from *Mefistophele*," *Callapooya Collage;*
"The Shirt," *A Good Man,* ed. Irv Broughton, Ballantine, 1995;
"First Fall," "Second Fall," "Third Fall," from "God's Pattern"; "Brother Cornelius," *Image;*
"Cantata for the Feast of Saint Anonymous" (as "Hymn for . . ."), "Discharge," "A Shift in the Wind," "Career Changes," and "Condemned," "Friend," "Sermon for the Women," "Pietà," and "Miserere" from "God's Pattern," *Poetry Ireland Review;*
"Woman at a Window," *Cimarron Review;*
"Samarkand," "The Aviaries of Dr. Harbinger," *Poetry Northwest;*
"Miami *Ars Poetica*" (as "Sunday in Miami"), "Self-Portrait, with Masks," *Shenandoah;*
"Sea Writer," *Cyphers.*

"The Gingriad" was published in a signed and numbered looseleaf edition by Crabapple Press, Spokane, Wash., 1995.

Contents

A Farewell to His Poems

Go, little gnats, little clever jackdaws, take
Off, you overdressed parrots, get out of my sight,
Not another word, with your coughs and hiccups,
Signals to your accomplices—after all
Those checks and corrections—go on, get what
You can while you can. You weren't meant

To turn out this way. I had in mind a play
Of light and sense, a dance, a leap, but demons
Possessed you as you took shape. Don't blame
Me when you go out in the world as runts,
As stammering badgers. How could I raise
Such a brood of foundlings, buzzing and prattling
And squabbling under my roof, and send you off
In style, trim, well-spoken, mannerly?

Well, go now. I won't regret the mouths I had
To feed so I could get you on your way if you
Can bring a moment's pause to one foe, one careerist,
One crawthumping bigwig hypocrite. Only a father
Could love you, my poppets, my treasures, hostages
To many a dark and doubtful hour. Go, you're free,
You changelings, to live on your wits, to leave me
Like this and take all I have—go where you must—
But never let on you're mine.

Holyhead

Here he is on an island
Where many an exile before him
Spent vain tears waiting
For the ferry over Lake Regret
To the last place he wanted to die in.

Now again the cliffs,
Rocks and flying spume,
Accents that slit the air
Like knives in silk,
The sniff of contempt for the alien

Who, in that world with its engines
Of contempt and envy
That urge *Get on with it or get out,*
Is not wanted anywhere.

So he settles for the one place
Back where he started,
Hinted at in his horoscope,
Not far over water,
Where he knows he can't stay.

A Famine Field in Kildare

for Mick Moloney

I Castletown House

October gales have stripped the beech-tree copse
Of every leaf, but yew and box keep their lines
Along the lawn. The largest house in Ireland,
Palladian façade and colonnade
Sweeping to embrace a southern prospect.

A palace really, built by a *nouveau riche*
Dealer in lands, a lawyer-politician
Risen to Speaker of the Irish House
Of Commons. The scale intended to celebrate
The way we think about harmony
As the measure of Man confronted by
Chaotic clouds and branches tossed in a gale.

II Celbridge and Maynooth

Autumn here, what you call "Fall" where you are.
Through the avenue's tall limes the fog drifts
In shreds from the Liffey, lingers on drenched fields.
Celbridge's main street, framed by the great stone gates
At the end of the avenue, is empty save
For the newsagent's grayhaired wife
Taking in the papers the van has left.
Far off, the high-pitched bell at Maynooth,
The highest spire in Ireland, straight as a nail
Driven into the irreverent gray sky.

3

These little Kildare towns, these ancient pastures,
Brace themselves against their history,
Expecting every ripple on Liffey or Boyne
Or crisis of state to bring them ruin or shame,
As when the Fitzgeralds' fortunes rose and fell
From castle keep to Dublin Castle cell. . . .
Now in the misty sunrise they're getting ready
To pray the Mass, to see what's in the news.

III A Famine Field

Celbridge will soon reach Maynooth on the road
Along the edge of Speaker Conolly's demesne.
A shopping-center on one side; on the other, small
Houses, cars bright with dew in the drives.
Across from the shops, a space walled in from the houses:
A little field, that keeps a strange repose
Beside the busy road, a step below
The asphalt. The grass so green.

A few yards in, a Celtic cross, no more
Than a child's height, the kind you'll see on graves
In every cemetery, modest imitations
Of those crosses the early monks raised, shaped
So that the circle of the heathen sun
Embraced the cross of everlasting life,
Golgotha's cross, put here when bones were found
As they began to build the new estate,
What you call, where you are, "development."

Roses and fruit trees leafless, gardens keep
Their backs turned from the field, the sunken grave

Of hundreds who died of what our flesh is heir to—
A few had tried to eat the very dust
Their flesh returned to in this piece of ground.

IV Conolly's Folly

Maynooth's chimes die away. The sun's weak light
Spreads silvery veils across the dripping roofs.
A drover shouts his cows down a muddy lane.
Conolly's Folly, an absurd mirage,
Floats over ragged hedges where the stately park
Once reached north two miles from the tall windows
Of the Long Gallery, the vista closed
By this memorial, an obelisk
Rising above arches, niches, urns,
Triumphant in its way, though not as tall
By any means as Maynooth's spire. The work
Of building it, the guidebook says, "created
Employment during the severe winter of 1739."

The house is being restored, a Heritage House:
Italian murals, crystal chandeliers,
Silk drapes and tapestries, a carved bed
Where a noble dowager is said to have died
As wretchedly as any whose bones are tumbled
Under the small cross in the famine field.
For a small fee, you can tour the lovely rooms.

V Where You Are

Many who could flee the famine's scourge,
Who witnessed silence fall like a wintry fog

Over the leafless woods and the blighted fields
Before they took their chances in a coffin-ship—
Millions found their way to where you are
After all hope was gone. When you come back to find
Your family roots, ask for the famine field.
There's likely one in every parish, or corner
Of some great estate, now ruined, the land dispersed
To tenants who survived to stake their claims.
Not everyone can tell you where they are,
Nor want to; but you can tell: the darker grass,
The sunken ground. No one can tell for sure
If anyone of yours lies buried there.

A Shift in the Wind

for Dave & Beth Britt

We keep heaving forward at first, though the shifting wind
Begins to jig in the mainsail, flapping it happily,
Tilting us over and round on our own wake,
And the leeward gunwale sinks into seething foam,
And the jib empties and ripples and we lose
Speed. The hand on the tiller wants to push
Angrily round off the wind; we'd lug and yar,
Reel and keel downwind to a slithering standstill
Like a sternstopped plough in its furrow. But you reach
To release the mainsail, jam over the rudder, and we jibe
Like an elegant drunk at a wedding dance, giddily
Balanced on the liquid floor, waltzing that woman,
That fickle Old Lady whose presence we know
From the sail's belly filling, her laughter in the rigging.
We cinch all the lines, check everything, lean back and let her go.

Waiting Room

from *Hospital*

Pursuant to their respective professions,
God, Death, the Devil, and St. Jude
Were sitting around in the Waiting Room, late one night.

"God is good," God said, not letting on
Who he was. The Devil smiled
At him in sympathy.

"Great and good and merciful," St. Jude
Added, without looking
At anyone in particular.

The Devil smiled at St. Jude also.
"Indeed, indeed," he murmured.
Death got up and left the room

And went to the third floor to take
The infant who, they said, was out of danger;
And to the fifth floor, and put

The old Indian out of his misery;
And to the O.R., to put a stop
To the brain-dead biker's revival.

He left the evangelist comatose
In the I.C.U., and rejoined the others,
Who were reading old issues of *Time*

And drinking coffee not fit
For human consumption. He addressed
God first, explaining the biker's innocence.

To Jude he made a special plea,
For the plight of the old Indian, a pagan,
Weighed on his conscience. To the Devil

He said, "Lucifer, God's own fool, the child
Is yours." The Devil complained, "Ah, now,
What would I want with a child? The biker'd be

More in my line." God, still believing
He was *incognito,* frowned and raised
A pointing finger. "God will decide. You know

Not the day nor the hour." St. Jude, who knows
The odds against everyone and picks the long shots,
Went over on that account to take

Death's skinny hand in his own plump fist
And blabber gratefully, "As long as even
One of these can be saved from doom

By a miracle with my name on it,
My job here's worth the trouble."
He wasn't sure what official part

Death played. God rolled his eyes to heaven.
"Wait now," the Devil fumed, "I'm the joker
In this pack. Take back the baby and play

By the rules. I'll wait for the evangelist
To croak." "Ask God," said Death, "He's here too."
"Damn it," God protested, "you've no right.

I'll reveal myself when the time comes."
Death did not stay to argue,
But went again on his rounds.

Dry Well

for Clare and John Keeble:
November 1996, the Ice Storm

This thin line
plumbs the well
stirs up
silted dregs
now we try
near day's end
paper and pen
the same old rite
trying to
make some sense
to draw down
God's will
for the pail
to fill even
a muddy brew
would remind us
of the saint who
dredged this spring
sipped the cool
grainy mix
of seed and dew
and declared
it wine

Triptych

I You Found Me

After sex and a little sleep, you found me half-
Erect at your bed again, bending down to you
As you awakened from a dream and we grew
The tulip in the rose again. Now you can laugh,
Recounting this nervously as we cross under half-
Naked maples, our feet dragging leaves. We knew
Nothing would come of it, didn't we? Yet I rue
That loss, the passing years, and when your laugh
Cuts memory from its mooring, old desire
Wears this absurd mask, as if you drew white-hot
Steel from my ribs. I wait as you unlock the car
And drive away. The low October sun burns
Shadows into asphalt. The years have taken turns
Plunging these daggers in, drawing them slowly out.

II You Are Unloved

You are unloved, though beautiful. Men
In your arms, enfeebled by your ardor,
Can feel on your breast the armor
Of old wars, and shrink from the pain
Of defeat. Some raise you to goddess, though
They risk this pain. Your eyes, dark gems
Of guile, leave your lovers with dreams
Which drain their very souls. They grow
Ashen, seared by your kisses. In my turn
I have joined those legions of night who spurn
The proffered gift. When you haunt the sky

Itself, we feel the full moon's burn,
We suffer the new moon's horn
Hooked in our bowels. You dare not lie
With any mortal suitor—he would uncover
Your unhealing wound. You need a god for lover.

III You Have False Friends

You have false friends. They tell you to your face
How beautiful you are. They praise your ivory skin.
They don't try to heal your grief. They speak the plain
Language of hypocrites. They praise you for the grace
You coddle us with, while you flit among us at the pace
Of a secret agent. They praise you for the sin
Of smiling pride, though you play with constant pain,
Watch your friends from friendship's quick embrace,
Keep to the rules of the oldest parlor game
So you may hoard every silly fawning smile
As a prize. In spite of you, I hunger to become
Your *honest* lover, the fevered heartbeat you feel
When you lie with me. But you yearn for some
Glory to wear like new skin, and wish us dead, one and all.

Breathing

He dived from the old stone wall
Into waist-deep water, and began
A slow overarm crawl, for maybe

A hundred yards. Stopped, out of breath,
And stood up. The tide pulled sand
From under his feet. He kicked

Off again, the rolling crawl,
Head down, up for air, shoulders
Rolling, arm stretched to pull down

The water under him, then the head
Rising sidelong again, one eye
On the shore, for it was steep

And he feared getting out of his depth.
He tired, and let his feet float down,
And began to sink slowly out

Of the glazed rippling light. He thrashed
With his hands and broke a gray roar—
His feet touched—he pushed up—

His lungs filled
With a huge element
A hacking that burst

From his open mouth to crack
A liquid mirror and he slipped down
Green ropes he tried to grasp.

His speech crusted with brine
When he tried to call out
How little it took to die,

How little it meant. The deep gods
Roared merrily and danced.
His feet felt sand. He tried to dance.

The Sorrowful Mysteries

In memory of my sister, Anne Weldon, 1934–99.

All I want, our mother would say,
Is peace, and turn away
From her canticle of grief
To change water and flour into a loaf.

Her muttering retreat, that house.
Her humors worked their leaven
Into waves of heat that rose
Round her at the oven.

Old songs and calamitous oaths
Were part of the daily office:
Jesus Mary and Joseph
Cursed, or could profess

Shaken faith. For the rosary
Old Mary, her thick-and-thin friend,
Joined the giggling family.
When the whiskey was at its wits' end

And the cash and credit low,
Piety got its turn: prayer
Lifted her spirits from woe
And gave Christ back his share.

The Shirt

I stole my father's shirt upstairs and passed
The busy kitchen without being stopped.
Out in the garden I pulled it on,
My white chasuble, to say Mass.

A backless kitchen chair served as altar
Against the wall that brought the sky
Down to the apple trees. I raised leaf-host
And jar-chalice in consecration.

The sleeves fell back to my elbows. I blessed,
Genuflected, mumbled offerings.
When Mass was over, I carried the Souls of All
The Faithful Departed between steepled fingers

Back to my mother in the steamy
Flagstone kitchen. She laughed and scolded
In the same breath: the good white shirt
Spotted like a sinful soul.

Child, when you have a mind to raise your hand
And bless the transubstantiated world,
Take anything of mine you need to give
Memory flesh and blood, to change grief
Into a leafy garden, an apple tree.

The Sacrament of the Tablets

from *Hospital*

for Rubén Trejo, June 1997

On the ceiling of the Temple of Oblivion
A scrolled proclamation intoned, *Rise!*
And a shadow drew aside his veil of sleep.
Duly he rose. Upon the incensed air
That held his torso upright for the rituals,
It was borne in upon him that he should accept
The will of the priestess leaning over him.
He held his right palm level out and there
Discerned a slight weight when she pressed the two
Tablets, intoning sacred mantras, *Take these*
For pain, and drink. Take these, and sleep.
After her benediction—*There, now*—he lay back
Into sheets of clouds and, a saint astray,
Drifted through temple precincts until he came
To a hall hung with filmy membrane, rose and pearl,
And he started humming, weightless, in the shell
Of light descending through the incensed air
From the ceiling in the Temple of Oblivion.

Brother Cornelius

Prologue

He shuffled in his woolly silence
Down the vaulted cellar passage.
Candlelight led him up the slanted curve
Of limestone steps to glowing waxed parquet,
The corridor's tall doors. At the chapel arch
He quenched his candle and entered a honeyed radiance.

The monks knelt in their stalls, bent toward the tabernacle.
He took his place. Incense thrilled his senses. He dozed
Until a brother touched his shoulder. They filed past,
Mouths hollowing and closing on their anthem.
He followed them in the rich incensed silence.
He heard no sound, so he made none.

Chapter One

The priest, his mouth a cave, his eyes ablaze,
Pressed his red hands hard on the boy's ears,
Glared up at God, shook the boy head-to-heels,
Rocked him back and pushed his face up at God.
The boy's eyes filled with tears. The priest glared down,
Waited the length of a prayer, then dropped the boy
And turned his back, his Redemptorist cloak
Swirling out through the incense fumes. The boy's
Mother appeared to him through his tears and took him away.

After the healer's failure, he seldom left
The farmhouse where his mother worked. She signed
To him of dangers waiting: the silent onrush
Of a car on the road, the town bullies, the ones
Who, like the priest, would turn their backs.

She taught him to churn butter, and paddle it
Into yellow bricks, to help her set the table
And carry in the soup without spilling a drop.
He scattered grain for the barnfowl, and sat
On the back doorstep watching their wattled heads
Drilling and snapping as they quarreled over
The seeds that lodged between the cobblestones.

Slowly, with letters that coiled along the lines
In his copybook, he formed words. He made
Dog. Cow. Hen. He drew a wattled hen
Beside the word. His mother hugged him.
She was round, and smelled of new milk
And floorwax, and her own sharp sweat.

Lamplight woke him when the narrow face
Of the thin girl from the other part of the house
Came to his attic room and pulled back
His blanket. She stared. Frowned. She frightened him.
She put her hand on him. Rubbed him. He arched.
There was an exquisite burning. He reared away.
Her frown. Then a brighter lamp behind her.
Her mother's thin ghost clawed and scratched.
He pressed into the wall, kept his eyes closed tight.
Then his round mother in her white nightgown
Signing to the girl and her mother, her mouth working.

Chapter Two

The rocking train made him dizzy, sick.
Tears rolled to gather in the corners of his mother's
Tightlipped mouth. He vomited a butter-yellow fluid.

She found work in a house with a shiny brass plate
Under the brass knocker: the doctor's name,
And SURGERY. Two-by-two the tall houses stood
Behind old sycamores along the wide street,
Their windows blinded with starched white lace.

He couldn't stay with her. They took him out the road
In the doctor's black humpback Ford, down a narrow drive
Lined with fragrant lime-trees, to the Home.
In a big room with eight beds, one was his.
They tried to teach him the language of the deaf,
But he was slow to learn, confused
By his mother's signing. He wrote words and drew
Pictures to make stories in his copybooks.

He gave them to his mother when she came
On her half-days off to bring him to the cinema,
Then the tearoom for cream-cakes and lemonade.
In twilight they dawdled along the road to the Home.
He'd watch her walk back to the high wall's corner,
Then wait for darkness before he'd go inside.

Deep in his throat a strange hoarse howl
Started and choked when they let him see
His mother laid out in her white flannel gown,
Her cheek so cold, the coffin waiting

On the floor by her bed. This the only sound
Anyone has ever heard from him.

He knelt when they knelt, fingering the beads
They put in his hand, but he would not stay
To see her lifted into her coffin, nor walk
Behind it from the church to her grave.
He stayed in the curate's parlor till they came
To take him back to the others. Their stares. Their signs.

Chapter Three

Another rocking train. Bare tree-limbs, black on gray
Clouds, made rushing patterns on the rain-streaked window.
Later, he would cherish these shapes. He dozed.
The rocking ceased. Then someone was shaking him, pointing
At two brown figures nodding to him from the platform.

They took him in the jostling pony-and-trap
A long uphill jogging jaunt through misted fields.
The dark came down the mountain to meet them.
The lantern jigged at the pony's rump till the wheels
Scattered the gravel of the abbey's forecourt.

Icy first light in high windows,
The chapel a frigid cave. Then the kitchen
All steam and glitter where he chopped and rolled
And sprinkled and kneaded and peeled the food
For meals three times a day, then scrubbed and splashed
Happily till all was clean and glittering at day's end,
When he could join the others for their prayers,
Kneeling in the chapel's honeyed glow.

CORNELIUS he painted in white letters
On his cell door, as he was shown to do.
After three years, prostrate on the marble step below
The altar in the gilded warmth of many candles,
He was received as Brother by the Abbot,
Who lifted him to his knees and signed the cross
On forehead, breast, and shoulders, then embraced him.
That night at prayer he felt his heartbeat thudding
In his veins. On his cot, he joined his hands on his breast
As he had seen his mother on her deathbed.

His Abbot wrote, *He's the hardest worker we have,*
And gave him more work to do. The great vat
Of tallow in the chandlery fretted his nostrils
All day while he was dipping string for tapers
Or ladling wax into molds for Paschal candles
Which he studded with patterns of colored glass
And carved with figures he copied from old books.

Chapter Four

On steel masts and pine poles the looped wires sang
As they crossed the valley and bounded along the hills.
Crews in all weathers advanced to take the land's
Measure and stretch the lines over rivers and bogs,
Up pasture slopes to slice a rift through the wood
That sheltered the abbey from the western gales.

Lights so bright they scorched his eyes. The chapel
Hardened, a gaudy barn. The Virgin's gown
A cheap blue wrap, the serpent a green joke at her feet.
He wrote in his careful hand, *Father Abbot you need*
No more candles. Give me new work. Cornelius.

Chapter Five

The monks crowded into the tallow-vat's reek;
Their mouths shaped alleluias.
The Abbot came in his poplin chasuble
With the gold embroidered letters, IHS.
A Brother swung the thurible; another bore
The processional crucifix. Cornelius knelt.

The Abbot raised his arm and blessed the four
Corners of the chandlery, then blessed the chandler
Before raising him from his knees. Then the procession
Down the vaulted passage, up the curved stairs,
And along the corridor into the chapel.

Not garish bars of light, but the honeyed glow
Of candles in the altar candelabra
And the sconces on the walls below the paintings
Of the Stations of the Cross. The Virgin's statue
Stood modestly in its shadowy niche. The Abbot signed,
The library must use the stronger light.
Electric power will help our other work.
We have machines to milk cows, churn milk!
Now he made more candles than they needed,
And sent them, packed in sheepswool, around the world.
In basilicas, cathedrals, pilgrim shrines,
The candles burned for great feast-days, or lit
A Zambian missionary's hut for Mass.
Once, in Rome, for Easter, before Pope John,
Cornelius's bejewelled candle glowed.

Now he could follow the Holy Office with his finger
On the page, while the others worked their mouths
Like fish. He still fell into reverie
At times, until he felt the hand on his shoulder.
Then he would rise with his brothers and shuffle
Up to his cell, where he would lie, hands joined
On his breast in the coffin-dark, until first light.

Lifebird

from *Hospital*

An awkward thing this from nose to tail, a craft
As noisy and misshapen as a flying tadpole, designed
In the worst of taste as a magic windmill to lift
Straight up from Emergency and grind
The air from here to there to fetch back
Humpty-Dumpty from under his wall, or George
From his dragon. Now we're up again, neck-and-neck
With a tragic ending as this one's eyes grow large
With a fast-forward story that passes understanding.
We take him down for the surgery as gently
As gravity will allow for a safe landing.
With the rotor's halo above him he must feel saintly,
If he feels at all, for he's getting ready to die,
The way he stares up from the stretcher, eyes all sky.

Cantata for the Feast of St. Anonymous

In the manner of J.S. Bach, Komm, du süsse Todesstunde

I Chorus

Now that we know how you spent
Your last days in the Jefferson,
The room overlooking the bus station,
We thank you for your death,
Which caused us the least trouble
Though we can't seem to get your
Skull-tight skin out of our minds,
Your fingers whispering on the gray
Frets of the coverlet.

We thank you for your death's repose,
Your drowsy gray eyelids,
Your blue lips, gap-tooth mouth
Half open, not a stir of breath.
You made your life in your own
Likeness, to make us grateful
For ours, while we slip your death-box
Into its pit with the pair
Of suicides from the river,
And our shovels flatten the good
Topsoil over the three of you
With rib-cracking thumps.

II Tenor

Yes, you slipped into this world
As helpless as you left it.
Yet, as a child, you had visions

Of a figure whose image, no more
Than a shadow, or a shape worn in stone,
Could leave you weeping: a bony head,
Deep-socketed, triangular,
On its little squared-off trunk,
Arms raised in praise or surrender,
A stiff likeness of what you became
As you made your life suit your death,
For which we thank you.

III Antiphon

   Chorus:
Mere stones called, and you obeyed.
You stepped close to a kind of glory.
Your fear offered others your faith.

   Tenor:
False judgement puffed you up:
Lovers were frolicking brutes.
The meek deserved their squalor.
These themes clothed your anger.

   Chorus:
As the seasons passed, you gave
To the rich too great a share
Of your esteem. You taught your children
The miser's names for virtue.
Children of your self-will,
They refused your stone-deaf god.
You started to descend,
Step by step, your terrace of woe.

Tenor:
Seen at home, perplexed,
Under the ruined fruit-trees.
Seen parked by the beach
At sunrise, hunched
Over the wheel, passed out.
Seen leaving the weedy lot
Wrapped in your overcoat, shivering.

IV Chorus

You spoke to no one of
Your soul's terror
In the absolute
Silence after prayer,
That blank iconic gaze.

The family you abandoned:
They knew. You were sure they knew.
They called you The Petrified Man,
The Speaking Stone. You amused them

With your Coptic truisms—*Be still
And know. In silence is truth.*
How had three decades worn
That youthful vision down
To the dust you stood in
While you waited to climb
On the Greyhound heading west
From Denver to make a new start?

You began to arrange for your death:
A grim lumber-mill town

Where despair slumped afternoons
In doorways. Day and night,
The sirens. No work, cheap wine,
The taverns a drumfire of complaint.

VI Tenor

Faded plaid shirt and workpants
Stripped from you and burned.
You stayed in the morgue three days,
The death-grin already fixed
To your skull while we made boxes
For you and the other two.
The city's road crews used their back-hoe
To dig us a plot to bury you in.

VII Antiphon

    Chorus:
We praise and thank you, who suffered
For a vision you couldn't endure.

    Tenor:
Your death will transform our fear
Into the peace you promise.

    Chorus:
Your struggle is ours
And our death, as yours,
Will bring truth to our children,
Our infidel children. For your death,
We thank you and praise you.

A Meditation, With Distractions

("Morgen," Richard Strauss)

A libidinous light flickers.
A trickle of trilling sound: a song–
Sparrow in the garden remembers
Arias from a well-favored opera
And spills a phrase or two
Into the morning from the evergreens
Which defend the garden from the suburbs.
Now warming air plays on the brow,
The sparrow's lean piccolo gives way
To a radio voice, *O Lord*
Deliver us, ever reminding us
Of Comedy's rueful promise
For the living and dying which we all
Expect another to do for us
When the evil we need to be
Delivered from slips up on us
As we sleep or wake, snug or stuck
In some awkward scene or in
The brooder's miasma of light airs
And grace-notes rippling from the *arbor*
Vitae. Pianissimo. Langsam.

Comely chords and harmonies crowd into
The citadel the mind insists on making up
For the spirit's stillness, a whispering empire
No better than the dead grass and doghair
Of the sparrows' palaces in shadowy hedges
That sever neighbor from neighbor, light
From the mind locked in its battle with

The warriors of leveling lust, as in the Crusades
Prayers were hurled like spears, spears like prayers
No matter what side God was on for the time being,
No longer deigning to play redeemer—though *that*
Is yet a useful idea, a breath away
From making the right connection—

A screech. The kettle! Heaven's wrecked.
Towers, domes, steeples gurgle in the teapot.
Badly scratched ideas float in the headlines,
The lies, hungers, betrayals of the *Times*
Spread like marmalade on toast. I'm teased
By the prospect of Prospero's echo

Of Philomel's echo at Her Ladyship's
Dainty earlobe, whereto I bend my lips,
Having brought the tray to her bedside;
Thence to her clavicle's but a semi-colon;
Twenty centuries have passed
Between the ears before the teapot's scalded,
The toast buttered, the tray fondly arrayed.

Magus and Brahmin, dolt and dreamer—
All understand these distractions.

When the Corpse Directed the Funeral

Everyone and his mother turned up. They all
Knew him well from the old days, by their own accounts.
The atmosphere was cheerful, one might say carnival,
But no one got out of line, or gave the slightest offense.

A Brother sang "Amazing Grace" in a pleasant Irish tenor.
A colleague from the Department told amusing anecdotes
Illustrating his quirks. Then the usual kind thoughts
About his tolerant patience, patient tolerance, generous demeanor.

Wine and tea after, with seed-cake the neighbor baked,
The talk turning to the latest events at home and abroad.
Later, old Uncle Frank got footless drunk and bored
The company with ditties and crude jokes. Each could take

Some little keepsake—a book, a picture, a necktie—as they left
To cast his ashes on the waters and the wind's light breath.

God's Pattern

Meditations on the
Stations of the Cross,
With Distractions . . .

I Condemned

Hung there above
The nuns, you,
Red drops like darts
On your white outsides.

That scared boy I was
Knelt in sin, clumsy
Street kid laced into
Boxing gloves to show off
The silly arts of self–
Defense to beaming mothers
At the convent drill display.
(Whose mother was too sick
To come? Whose d'you think,
Jackass?) Red drops, real blood
On a white shirt when the round
Ended with the Angelus Bell
And rosary novenas on scraped knees
Benched before the thorn-crowned martyr-god.

Blood, blood, blood. The son
Tugged swathed in red
From the mother's womb
Soon learns cut-and-thrust
Wounds in a scrape with gang-boys

All along Church Street—gouts of it,
Streams, streaks, gobs of bloody offal
Over the slaughterhouse floor
Where we peeped in, straggling home
From bloody McGinty's bloody
Sixth Class National School.

II Scourge

Flesh. Flesh of the sweaty hand,
Flesh of calves and hams,
Flesh waltzing the path across from him,
That fag-dangling, mouth-agog youth I was,
Gaping after the Woman of the Town,
Flesh of round bubs and bum, Bridie.
For five quid, they said, she'd haul
His ashes for him—she'd tempt
That whipping snake to dance
Hilarious down his veins—

That sin-stained altar-boy I was,
Eager to be tormented more
By the wish for a whisk of a high warm wind
To strip Big Bridie of every stitch,
Reproduced in glossy *Mayfair* and *Men Only,*
Unholy magazines from dirty London
That found their way home
In unholy Father's flightbag.

III Cross

Vertical:
the sun's
bright side.
Vertigo reels the globe through
its paces. Try to lift your head.
The crowd's
pulsed voice
draws you up
the cobbled
lane. Friends,
encmies,
urge you,
need you
erect here
to begin
the way

IV First Fall

To know yourself, *he said,*
And took me to my knees
With the weight of his lesson,
At your worst and best, *he said,*
Is to contemplate, *he said,*
This dirt, *he said,*
With your worm's eye, this
Humus you're made of, not
Whole, not sound enough
To be fearless face-to-face
With the dark loam,
Without friend or enemy.

V Mother

What laws, whose laws ordain
Your suffering when your son
Brings on himself this pain?
I could blame Miss Fortune,
The grizzled crone behind
The counter of her mean
Little sweetshop in Hand's Lane.
She robbed the children blind
And we robbed her to get our own
Back on the hucksters of the town,
Those grayfaced hoors, *Bless 'em all,*
The long an' the short an' the tall. . . .

You must have told me often
I was forgiven, but I could hear
Only those rhymes to soften
The darkness you sang, the rare
Ineffable flight of your singing
The flesh and blood of my beginning.

The couplet on your gravestone
Had to wait until great wordstorms
Blew themselves out on the wall
Of my pitchcap stubborn skull
And death and I could come to terms
With all that's done and left undone.
Now from the prison of my will
You are released, so that your son
Lifts his own burden with his own arms.

VI Friend

A word from you   and you
Would lighten   what dark holds
Between   the bruised hills
My shoulders make   so I share
Your horizons   and the bleeding
Clouds   behind my back

But pardon   I don't make
Sense even   when you ask
For a simple   word of truth
Rather a rain   of blows
Than this   argument
Between self   and soul
O pardon   pardon   pardon

It is made   this plain   cross
Of words   I always   hear
From you   this fear   I can't help
You to end   this round   of words
It won't   close on   any sense
But which   tell me   which whips

Worse   the word   you help
Me with   or the long   agony
Between   horizons   of waking
In the spirit   or the body's   night?
Help me   now   the next
Step   pushes   under my feet

       You   I have   long ago
Pardoned   you made   that easy
From   the very first   you who did
Me no wrong   take this   next step
With me   it is   so hard

VII Veronica

She who loves me is not loath,
When I battle to no avail
Lunging at that old windmill death,
Trying to turn aside his tireless flail.

She who keeps my mortal secret
Holds before me a veil of doubt.
Death turns to face me. She in sacred
Blood has written my secret out.

I go forward a cruel step.
Cruelty follows close behind.
She whose love would ever keep
Me safe from death has left this sign.

Another step. I fail again.
Her veil is my mask of life
When death rounds on me again,
The seventh sense that feels love's knife.

VIII Second Fall

Simon says *Fall down*. Oh friend, don't come here
Where every pebble's a hill and weedy grass
Mimics a jungle cave where Prospero and Lear
Argue with Fate and nymph and satyr caress
Under a nettle's shade. To whatever gods are near,
Hidden behind the sky's gray veil, I confess
Unless you lift the skull-heavy load I haul
I may not rise again, though ants beckon, crickets call.

Brain. Membrane. Blood. Breath. Hindsight blinds,
Deafens me. The clever construct of skin, the ooze
Of venery, the wound of love open to the mind's
Fervor, the howls of grief, betrayal, the lewd vows
Paid to anyone who'd lick my dusty wounds—
With every word, a lie drifts into silence. The news:
God Bites Man. Blind with dust of flesh, the gore
Of an ill wind, I kneel. Silence. I need you more,

Friend, than air. Simon says, *Take up again
Your sane semblance*. Easy to obey
When the heart listens. Am I Abel or Cain
When cock's a-hoop and ta-ra-diddle rocks
The cradle? But what's enough? It's plain
Our mother's wound's a word and words decay
To dust. Or worse, her tears return to flesh
And blood runs out her man-making gash.

Graceless I fell from mother-arms; from all
That fall the tears turn into blood. The fame
Of fall is the rising from. I hear you call,

Mother of all, and feign a rise, but the name
Of one whose word's enough to make dust crawl
Upright on this hill of sorrow will come
Only to lips unsealed by the mortal kiss
Of flesh on flesh. Without that word, the abyss.

IX Sermon for the Women

Today the old man who smothered his wife
    went free. This was mercy.
Today the troops who burned in their tanks a week ago
    made a rubbery stink in the desert.
Today the infantry recruits capered
    like marionettes before the cameras.
Today a drunken senator snored
    while a woman screamed for help in his garden.
Tonight the woman from Ecuador sleeps with three children
    under the freeway ramp. Her man is working nights
    stacking shelves in a Miami supermarket.

Today two brokers agreed on a price;
    twelve hundred workers met in a hall and voted.
Today the editors blessed our leaders for ending
    the week's war. Sheik and emir returned
    to their desert palaces.
Today six thousand barrels of toxic sludge
    were unloaded from barges in Dakar.
Today the cop pumped thirty slugs into the heart
    of the man-size target, for practice.
Tonight they buried a child on the Kurdestan mountain
    while her mother bathed another's fever. Her keening
    rose higher than the blustering helicopters.

Today the deacon fingered the choirboy's anus;
    the pastor wrote out check after check
    in the presbytery.
Today the brawny oiled-up hermaphrodite posed
    and pranced before the gymnasium mirrors.

Today the grayhaired man, who knew this woman
    seven years, punched her, raped her,
      then apologized.
Today three men who professed to love peace
    sat in the city of peace and continued their quarrel.
Tonight the wife read a story
    that could be her own; the husband
    sat in his basement den, staring at nothing.

Tonight, a girl leaned back from the finished page.
    A deep breath. Then she leaned
    forward again into the light.
Tonight a woman felt the planets
    spin and wheel, wheel and tilt,
    and hummed their music.
Tonight you lift the child from his outcry
    and hold him to your breast.
Today these three who love peace are still
    on the long pilgrimage to peace.

X Third Fall

Ach! Tastes ill, this dust, its mortal bloody tang.
Let me drop at last under my weight of wrong.
Where I am fallen, false pity's patrons raise
Memories to stay me. Rub spittle into dust, and there's
Our ancient Father, frowning from on high.
Then he takes off in a cumulus of goodbye.
Father of my own making, step light and even.
Come and go light's way, so *I will be forgiven.*

With him the women, one with her worried frown,
The other fairly smiling; she on his left in a gown
Not much in fashion; she on his right all blue hues,
Glad as forget-me-nots. Handsome the one who does,
But lovely the one who gives. Neither is prized
For personal virtues. On this gray road beside
The striding father, wife and mistress have given
All and nothing for love, so *they will be forgiven.*

Close at their heels trail Brothers, Cousins,
Sisters, Uncles, Aunts, Nuns, Jesuits, dozens
To whom I feel obliged, for the tremor of a chance
Remark or toy or joyful insult, to commence
Resentment. Swallowed anger feeds on fantasy:
Dozens of bloodless enemies are murdered savagely
And sent unshriven to doomsday terrors. They can go
Now to a hell of their own making, or accept their due
Share of these ancient pains and so, of their own volition,
Pass into peace passing all *and be forgiven.*

How much longer can this long worm possess
Me, this carcass eat itself? What of the sweats
And stinks of lust? Greed's gruels and saccharins?
Advance to play and replay a thousand scenes,
One by one: Companion, Colleague, Contestant,
Prizewinner, Egotist, Superior. Let expectant
Self take the victim's role as you take turns to recite
How many ways I have badgered and hated you, spite
Riddling me while you gained Port Success
And my skiff drifted toward the venereal Rocks.

Father, free me from these creatures of the seven
Sins of my own making, so *I will be forgiven*.

XI Tango Magdalena

Tears glazed her eyes, like jade beads in water—
Real tears, though they deceived—a jade mirror
Of vacant heaven. Our fevered loving would sate her,
Then repentance. Oh how this plough could furrow
Her flesh with gasps and cries! Love levelled her, terror
Invaded her to the throat—ecstasy! Later
The edgy smile, the frenzy, the clawed spasm that tore her
Even in the hour of unbidden tears, her mood borrowed
From ancient adulterous myth. Those tears accuse
And then forgive. They spill on her cheek to slake
Anguished, relentless thirst. We began again with a kiss
And rounded the circle: Spring's looting tongue, Summer's ache,
Fall's bloody fruit, Winter's icy word, to use
In season, when she'll weep again for our sake.

XII Garment

Bad, friends. Angelic sidewise sidewinders have stripped
Those pretensions, those semblances you understand
As understandings: that I am man (for a moment, I crave
Your indulgence); that, as human, so divine I breathe soulfire,
Though I have let be stripped from me all that—out of desire
For the soul's nakedness—you know of me, you know me—not
As friend, nor as angel, nor as ripping wind—but as the snake
Uncoiling, whipping—whipped into surrender.

So now, the joke goes, as you know me
Without the insignia of voice, the clout of skin
Stretched on the bone drum, you want me to recover
A demeanor, some smile-mask or other, some wide-awake
Wide-open pain-mask howling for attention, for your
Forgiveness, the coil-uncoil of lying explanations
To allow you to see yourselves as friends in me
Here naked in the mirror of your forgiveness, to license
You to clothe me in your suffering,
To be Adam again for you
On your tree of shame.

XIII Ecce

Father, Father, who gave
Us this deadly flesh, why
Do you not wait close
Enough to hear? Did you
Give us this pain out of love,
This death of your speechless will?
Must I now let go
This likeness of you?

Poor body, you have used
Me for the cruel dances
Of drill sergeant and recruit,
Of drunken killer
And his hollow *daimon*.
How can I let go
Flesh and its shadow?

Poor brain, cage
Of reason, team captain, watchman,
Helpless witness to the strut
Of fame's cock-a-snoot
Half-hour to-do,
Here, I let go.

Why vex me with needs
And claims? Being one
With your multitude,
I take off this worn frame
Of self, emptied
So I may let go.

Cast me as a spoonful of dust,
Echo in a wine-jar,
Voice that cries day and night
Over avenues, suburbs,
Cornfields, powerplants. Father
I cannot know, claim me
Now I let go.

XIV Pietà

Enter the peace of the Mother of Sorrow.
Here is the womb's red silence.
Rest. Let her bear your weight.
Let her hold you in silence.

Behind, the labyrinth between lives,
The life given and the life taken.
Beyond, the dark path to the center.
Sleep in her wise silence.

She who holds you in life and death
To her heart, the figure for love,
Cold as marble, yet no betrayal,
Offers you, her child, her life.
With your last breath, the word for love
Takes form in her unfailing silence.

XV Miserere

Dark rises through stony ground.
From the hill the city spins
And reels with its mobbed streets.
Streaks of light wheel and flow.

The world narrows to a cave.
I am found in the same shape
I was born with: the Stripped Fool.
You who are called to believe

A shadow in a cave,
Take the stir of wind
Through grass as prophecy.
Take every breath as truth.

Samarkand

Daniel, the late-born, has brought us down
To the beach on his first holiday to learn
All there is to know of gullsky, seawind.
He stretches out his hand to the Pacific,
Rigid with a deep excitement. In a while,
We track through the dunes until we find
A sheltered spot behind a drifted log.

I want to teach him sandcastles, to work
With spade and pail and patience against the way
Sand loses itself in sand. But he shovels and sifts
To no purpose, as a gull wears the wind, and soon
Tires. You put him to your breast.
He plunges to an amniotic dream.

While he's beyond my tutelage, I toil.
A wall rises to stop a valley's mouth.
Many towers on the wall; a *motte* and *fosse;*
Unnumbered loyal defenders within. For miles
The crenellated fortress rises round
The new city. Towers, domes, a piazza laid
Open before the basilica, all declare
And measure the ruler's power, so while he sleeps
He prospers. A seer foretells he'll govern
With fair heart and even hand, and be called great,
And his capitol will survive the millennium.

He opens his eyes. He smiles. He shakes himself.
On all fours, he goes to inspect his kingdom.
One knee flattens a palace. A small fist sinks

Into a terrace, a temple, a triumphal arch.
He pushes forward, breaches the great wall.
All vanishes into sand that was an empire
For the golden age you nursed him and he slept.

Woman at a Window

She rested, or pressed, her hands
Against the sill on the second floor
Of the new townhouse. Below her
On the sidewalk a crowd streamed past
In twos and threes, whether for church
Or theater or protest march
She was not to know.

She wore an oldfashioned gray
Frock or blouse with a wide
Lace collar, her dark hair drawn
Back in a tight topknot that made
Her plain face an alabaster mask.

Neither hope nor despair in her pose.
Whether a lover would visit
Or family from out of town
Was not her concern. Her hair
Was a bronze lie in the evening light.

She leaned forward now. Her mouth,
Half-open for a phrase
From Schumann or a cry
Of greeting, was a soft plum
In a face made pale by waiting

For her fate, one could assume.
But when she stood straight
And turned back into the room

To answer a question, or bite
Into a ripe pear, or undo her hair,

She disclosed no tragic sign.
Yet some aspect of her form
(Her only chronicle)
Drifted in the idle stream
Of my thought as I passed

On the other side of the street,
And sent enough pity and fear
To draw the whole scene round her
Like the mantle of black lace
She might wear in the last act

Of a tawdry opera. The slanted light
Stitched details into a possible
Scene: a brocade gown, a table,
Candelabra. Her life could end
With this verse as her last aria. . . .

She crossed behind the window,
Now a shadow, which could belong
To anyone searching for peace
In the vision I retained
As she left my sight. A girl,

Blonde, twenty, left the building
And walked past me, a charmed doll.
Her passage too would end
In silent leavetaking. Then one
Woman would assume the other's life.

After a Chorus from *Mefistofele*

Slowly over arctic years ice inched between
Bare rock and carved its runes where now
Ivy sinews grip the sarcophagi and work
Lewd thumbs between the mortised stones.

Neglect of centuries, the flight of generations
To newfound continents, have left the winter-stiff
Yews that overhang the tomb to groan
In October's leaf-blizzards when they blow

Old nests, mousedung, nettleseed
Round the gravestones. Slow earth shifts and sinks.
Stone slabs crack, coffin-dust powders hair-tufts.
Disjointed heels and fingerbones find

The grave's new mouth of their own accord
And sidle out, conspirators who won't
Acknowledge one another in open air,
Imprisoned soon again in mud and roots.

Lichen and ivy and the snail's progress erase
Her name, and his, and their children's prayer
From the broken stone, so it means no more
Than the scored rocks left by the glacier, or

The prattle of rooks assembling in the oaks.
Eternity's a discordant background whistle
Among the broken tombs, the crushed nettles,
The dank ivy, where we have left our dead.

Winter Drive

On ice you try the brake
To keep a steady line
Where the road should go.

An element from behind,
Cunning as Caliban,
Guides you against your will

Forward broadside over
A confused drift at the center
Into the way we came.

You face the slanting snow
While the senses argue.
Cars sway past, a consort

Of sympathetic murmurs.
By keeping quiet, the cold
Persuades the heart to slow.

Now the eye accepts
The road's white retrospect.
Shivering, amused,

We make silence welcome.
When it's clear at last,
We ease round for home.

Miami *Ars Poetica*

for Donald Justice

Visiting your home town, I was instructed
And pleased by the skinny tramp who strutted
Shirtless along the yellow strip on N.E. First
Between growling buses, pants at the hipless waist
Held up by an unseen power, the same charm
That infused his gesturing famished arm
With eloquence while, without a word,
He urged an army forward. Then he cheered
A sulky boardroom up; then wheeled and raised
Both arms high and wide to accept our praise;
Then rested by the derelict Goodwill store. ¶Enter
His double from Flagler Street, staring down the center
Line, the dazzled drivers risking serious
Wreckage to avoid his progress. Delirious
Lest he spill the wine from the invisible chalice
Which his distrustful hands held in the balance,
He climbed up unseen steps to some priestly function.
¶ My Biscayne bus came. A pair of dwarves, at the junction
Of two important streets whose names I forget,
Boarded. They moved and amused me, one excitedly set
On keeping the other from getting too excited
About their trip to the Aquarium, where they exited.
¶ I paced the beach once paced by Ponce de León
And (closely guarded) the unimpeachable Nixon.
Wasn't it Horace who instructed us that delight
And instruction should balance and keep us straight
Lest we put a woman's head on the neck of the horse
We ride, up sky and down, pursuing Truth? ¶Of course
Alter Ego was at the bus stop for the ride back: a gassy drifter,

Three sheets to the inexhaustible wind, mistakenly gifted
With a grab-bag of comment on mores, politics, religion,
Delivered between beer-burps in a tone just shy of belligerent.
He'd picked up this wrong-headed data in the library
While sheltering from storms and the social weather. ¶Bribery
Kept him from bending my ear all the way back:
For a couple of bucks he left his place for another sack
Of beer, and another night under a sibilant palm-tree
With whose views he would, near sunrise, come to agree.

Recovery Room

from *Hospital*

Slip one breath
Into the next. Here
The only function's
Breathing. All in green
Goes my medico, one-
On-one with scope and chart,
Checking the vitals.

He's checking parts without
Feeling, or without the sense
To collect the ether signals
That say, *Feel that. Feel that.*
Nerves intimate sickly
Routines, indecent business
With offal-whiff, fear-groans, a slick
Eel-finger in a latex glove.

Who calls out these names?
Who could make up such names?
They mean great wounds, great
Afflictions. I steal away
Into unfeeling zones. Snap
Back into pain. Into great pain.

Attendants in green swaddlings
Steer their preoccupied gurneys
In and out of Nirvana.
Sooner or later, poor souls,
They get caught in body-traffic:

A chin tipped up on its neck
Like a foot without toes;
A clay-white foot on its heel
Like toes arranged on a chin.

Tongue works on sandy teeth.
But I've no need to converse
With my neighbor, the ghastly
Elder supine on my right.
He's the keeper of death's dirty
Little secrets, by his looks,

And has put some distance
Between his old friend Pain
And those *Vitals* they keep
Checking on the charts.

An ad hoc committee forms
For a meeting in my head,
The only hideout left
For the delegates from all quarters
To deliver their reports.

We've passed a resolution
To keep quiet till we're rolled out,
One way or the other, before
We protest the conditions here
Between one breath and the next.

Career Changes

I could compose cadenzas for disappointed wives,
Soothe them with psalms of eye-shadow and paring-knives.

I'll stay behind at the base-camp under the crags,
In charge of the meal-packs, unguents, body-bags.

Tramps will bring me the trinkets they don't need.
I'll exchange them for camphor and poppy-seed.

I'll deal from my strong suit, be the lawyers' coach.
I'll stuff tautology and hoodwink down their throats.

Black lingerie, eye-shadow: I cover the yawn with the smile
In pastel salons, where I'm the Girl With Guile.

I'll be the last clerk left in the bankrupt store:
Thirty-nine years on the *Chinoiseries* floor.

Politicos may find ways and means interesting,
But up in my glassy tower I'll do investing.

The Munich clown-god needs a cycling bassoonist.
A difficult performance, but I'm an opportunist.

Cardiac Arrest

from *Hospital*

a white   room   was rising
or falling   hard   to tell
a ringing   below   or above
no way   to be   sure
above   a fine   white shell
or vault   a dome   ivory
or bone   from below
slight   palps   the spine
or skull   now   the ringing
has eased   whispering
a long   sigh

many   in one   we were drawn
down   a roaring   tunnel
or cloister   and rose   into white
light   or no light   a high gale
or   silence   glory

now you   thunderous
pump in my ear
you   call me   back
to your   numb   fears
the aches   that reach   back
you   your red   thumping
fills   the white   room

Nude with a Calla Lily

Death-pale skin. Ribs
Carved into every breath.
Poor girl from the streets.

He will stroke the paint
In slow broad sweeps
Of ivory-white haunches.

The smooth white curve
Below her navel has him
Working hard while she

Surveys, dark eyes half closed
His world over her thin
Shoulder, her incurious

Calm, a sphinx ready
To ruin us with doubt.
The sun has given her arms

And face the warm hues
Of this flower, which dares
Her to turn the stem between

Her fingers, rip the hot
Orange spadix from its white
Hood, and start a war

That will flood the globe
With the heavy stench
Of its crushed flesh.

She keeps her pose, though.
The lily's no more than the idle
Detail at rest by her elbow.

Freed from her pose she will stretch
And close her eyes, her slight frown
Enough for the world he knows

To blaze with terror of what
She thinks of it. Before
He is finished he will fix,

In the umber shades behind her,
His own shadow like a rapist's
Waiting there while he studies
The pale blades of her hips.

The Aviaries of Doctor Harbinger

Controls. No, not cages—great barns,
Like plane hangars, on an offshore island.
Glass from roof to ground, and coated wire,
So the least harm would come to the birds. And trees,
Dunes, bushes, small lakes, a complete
Estuary—everything required
To reproduce the native habitat.
Funds? From the Pentagon, to study
Computer models for wing attitudes in flight,
Behavior under stress, all that. Of course
The work was useful in other ways. A few males
Grew duller plumage, females attacked intruders,
Some mated out of season. Raptors hunted less keenly
Over our prepared terrain. Most settled well.
We fanned wind through the trees at intervals,
A good blow to freshen the place, waft seed down
For warblers, finches. We placed the mockingbirds
So they'd hear nightingales—not crows—God forbid!
When the snow-geese caught a virus, we took measures
To keep the other species from infection.
We tried to ensure the outcomes would be harmless,
And we always used the minimum controls.

The moon's effect on egrets taught us something
About reversion, hysteria. In a word,
They went mad. Some type of alienation.
Squawked and flapped all night, disturbed the pelicans,
Flamingos, a whole week of that. We used
A mild sedative, a form of gas, finally,
To calm them down. That was in Sixty-four.

In Sixty-eight we sent vaccines in darts
To cure a disease in the crows, at my suggestion.
Another expedient: in Seventy-two we erased
A painted wall of clouds and greenery—our flock
Of rare Andean wrens had flung themselves
Against it, with some casualties. We introduced
Kiwi, ostrich, and emu into the area. Their
Stately flightless pacing restored peace.
But at the equinox—that cursed moon!

The answer to your question is not so easy.
Think of the data—on flight itself, of course—
But also on behavior, loyalties, motives.
The doves, so arrogant. The sad goldfinch
In its thistle-patch. The greedy old cormorants,
The opal-eyed Thai owls, who mated like bats.
The soldierly foraging sparrows. To improve
The curlews' lot, we altered the tidal area,
Which changed the heron and tern flocks
For the worse, a little. There are no easy answers.

We left the magpies and the rookeries,
And the neat nests of thrush and bunting—
How restless the swallows every season, dabbing
Mud from their beaks under our false eaves
To build their shabby homes! Larks, gulls, pipits,
Quail—whole armies of birds hardly bothered
With nests at all—and so much waste!
Eggs that crumpled between my fingers when
I lifted them from nests of matted twigs

In rotted logs—those cradles of Sodom! No,
We can't release those pampered creatures—sterile,
Many of them, anyway. When we withdraw
We'll leave them on the island. They're well adapted.
But the raw data's classified. It's complex.
They'll control themselves—each other—when we've left.

Delivery Rooms

from *Hospital*

I Mater

He remembers nothing definite: images
Of crimson pleasure, a pulse like rain falling
Over a sea-sweep. After he was born
He kept nothing down, and in six weeks was given
Up for dead. "We had a little white
Coffin bought for you," his mother explained
Between whiskey sips one cozy, dizzy evening
Two decades later, when tuberculosis
Had seized on both of them, and they were playing
"Down Memory Lane," that treacherous family game.

He imagines her in the Mater Hospital ward,
Herself a foetus, curled up and turned to the wall
So she wouldn't be made to leave the bed and see
Him dead in his cradle. She's foetal again now
In the wing-back armchair, nursing a Baby Power's.
"A medical student was sure you were a goner,
So he gave you a thump in the chest, to kill or cure you."
She chuckles and leans to the fire with the poker
Riddling the coals. "Ah, the smile and the tear. . . ."

II Pater

Fearing God, and much else besides,
In a fancy nursing-home for rich neurotics,
His first wife—who'd blame her?—did three days
And nights of hard labor before a forceps tugged

Their firstborn into the April evening when all
They owned was on the never–never, not
A moment to lose between the final demand
And the overdraft. The son named after the father
And the father's father, for all the good *that* did him.

She delivered their second quickly in Holles Street
And in the confusion lost her wedding ring.
Prayed to Saint Anthony and the ring turned up
In the bed under the baby boy who was given
The saint's name out of gratitude. Then they all
Went off to America, seeking a change in fortunes.

The third son named after Ireland's teenage martyr,
Kevin Barry, in a hospital far from the father
Who'd flown the coop which wasn't his scene since
He'd let his hair grow, drank too much, and split.
He should have gone back to them or been locked up,
And he deserved both. But it just wasn't his scene.
He drank at his ghosts, married again, moved on.

III Familia

Stern Owen, his fourth, blonde and princely, he spied
Behind the hospital glass. Then he gladly announced
The birth at the Saddle Inn, his home-from-home.
Drinks for his friends. Drinks on the house. Drinks.

Soft and cheerful, Rory arrived in May
Of another year, basked by the back door
Or nuzzled his mother while the father thought
In the manner of Berryman's mortal Henry of

How he could kill himself so nobody would notice,
So deep in loathèd Melancholy was he,
Also the heebie-jeebies and deetees,
The rasp of memory, and his old pal fear.
It took some years to climb up to humility.

IV Pace

Fathers in overbright waiting-rooms, the nervous
Flicker of TV News and Sport, the bravado
And terror of three A.M., when the mothers are wheeled
Into rooms where they scream and moan and curse
At doctors and nurses like witches at their sabbath—
Pace, fathers. Sit. Stand. Pace. Wait for the news
From the rooms that Artemis long ago
Decreed were sacred to childbirth and men were banned.

Fathers feel in the throat the older growl
Of hunters on wild slopes, knives in their teeth—
Or is it the cigarette smoke? Anyway,
Hunter and prey have vanished long ago.
Who would sing those psalms and ballads now
To their children? Half-forgotten tales
That once could summon *Creator Spiritus*
To house or hearth. Could he bring himself
To beg his children's pardon, make amends?

Someone has changed the channel. Salute, fathers,
Your mothers, and your children's mothers. Let
Your laughter be pleasing to the goddess, and amends
Will be made when the will is made to bend,

Now we're tuned to programs where fathers may
Attend the birth of children and suffer the shame
Of being useless when they're needed most.

V Spiritus Loci

Terror's voltage shocked him head to foot
And blasted every law of life and death
While witless he witnessed, forty hours and more,
His beloved in battle with his latest child
Who wouldn't surrender to the fact of his birth
Till the surgeon caesared the womb and held
Him high at the forty-first eleventh hour.
Daniel his name, for a brave man we loved well.
Eyes clenched shut, he bleated angrily,
Not pleased with his parents who nevertheless
Managed a kind of awe, a kind of glee.

They let him carry this astonishing son
To be weighed, labeled, and introduced to the world.
After the drug had released her into sleep,
He sat beside her bed and stared amazed
At her hand in his, and gave resentful thanks
To the feckless *Spiritus loci* of delivery rooms.

Sea Writer

I Sands

Sand is the history of shell and rock,
The changed word received from our forebears,
How it prevails, headland to headland, dune
To wave. *And* the gulls' mockery!

Sand has every right to arrange its own
Rhetoric, grind it as fine as it likes,
Even to mock its own definitions,
Its fame for taking time's measure with plenty left

To span a beach for the next ice age and more.
We can stand to admire it, or walk off on it.
Even its banality's worth remarking.
Come, walk with me as far as that green cliff.

Make anthologies of its gleams, the means
Glass uses to make metaphors. Its power
Will weave a silky skin round stones,
Although its cruelty may leave you blind.

You will show unlikely mastery
If you can say, precisely, fluently,
Sand, sand, sand, sand, sand.

II Tides

And you who bow to your work here and there
Under the headland, shielding your eyes with your hand

Betimes against the glare—no ancient rights attach
To your lifetime's devotion to wavelet and smooth rock,
So don't bark in your rough way, so famously "direct,"
About fishers, kelp-gatherers, driftwood-mongers.

Stay faithful to your impressions. Give them purpose.
The tides that broadcast your intentions are also your
Unruly editors, your disobedient caretakers,
Always ready to clear away your inventions.
Discover a prospect, a view, and in time you will change
All we thought we knew for generations.
But we distract you. Please, carry on with your work.

III Words

We traced these signs with stick or fingerbone
On the exhausted rock and shell to claim
No heritage, leave no memorial,
But merely to practice our sad craft, to teach
Kelp-gatherer and beachcomber how
Sand is matter, process, and *the word, a sign*
That sand is history, making none of its own,
Since the collapsing waters heave it into mere
Resemblances of greater meaning, afloat
Among the darker shapes of the breaking waves.

Walk in the Wild

The bald eagle presents its presidential
Profile, spreads one wing. The other's a stump.
"This zoo sucks," a fat child whines. "That bird,"
I lie, "Survived when a poacher shot it
For the feathers. Anywhere but here
It would have died." Many a moral tale
Depends on a lie. The girl slumps on a bench.

Heat has shrivelled the grass. A dappled fawn
Watches the visitors with liquid eyes
From the shade of a tractor–tire bedded in sand.
This is the children's corner, "The Petting Place."
Children fondle goats and lambs. Hutches hold
Piebald rabbits in close confinement. They flinch
From the children's reach; noses give moist warnings.
Tricks of the eye: nickels and pennies distorted
In a blue miasma where carp and catfish patrol
Round the islet confining the fox, so he won't molest
The dusty peacock who hides under a bush,
Common barnfowl for company, out of the heat.

More creatures will arrive as funds permit,
Announces a newsletter tacked up on a lightpole.
Fences are going up around rough ground,
Future homes for llama and giraffe.
The cougar will have a lair more to her liking
Than this crude shack and concrete patio
Where she sprawls on her side and paws idly at insects.

Kaiser Aluminum, whose plant across the river
Sits on this landscape like a tin hat on a goddess,

Has promised a grant when the recession eases.
They don't pollute the river on the surface
But the aquifer deeper down, the primal waters.
They help the Symphony, United Way,
Employ more workers than any other outfit.

Along a trail through a grove of ponderosa
We come to a duckpond under a low cliff
That sends a basalt echo, "Wait for me!"
It doubles as the buffalo's watering hole.
Now, here's a beast worth paying money to see,

A big prizefighter, dusty fur-collar coat,
Big shoulders and narrow loins—what a sight,
Great herds thundering over the prairie,
Winchesters barking and barking at their heels!
Isn't he a wonder, our dusty champ,
For a mother to ponder, her child calling, "Wait for me!"

The reptiles are disappointing. Motionless,
They curl behind the glass or lie along
Limbs sawn off from nearby pine or aspen.
More than the ancient sleep of snakes, the wood—
Worn to the grain into shapes that mock the gods—
Could visit hatred and fear on the children of Eden.

But the cockatoo cheers us up, old jungle trouper,
Outrageous in green and yellow finery
And gaudy nasal make-up. She performs
In the dusty heat, slow feats of balancing
And fetching, tongue clumsy as a thumb stuck
In her thick beak when her poker-face keeper pays
Her off with a peanut and she poses for photos.

By the exit, the owls. Their great gold eyes
Stare from the communal cage. One blinks
Glacially. The horned owl frowns in fury.
The gloomy screech-owl stares; the barn-owl's amazed.
Patient as gold, those eyes. The visitors cross
The parking lot and leave through the rippling heat.

Landscapes, with Interior

for Paula Cunningham

I Interior

One most beloved, the other our new friend,
Are seated together on the flowered couch:
A Vuillard scene. Their talk is as familiar
And as strange as my aunt and mother murmuring
Before the fire, heads askance in low light,
The mantel with its row of antique jugs,
Spode, Derby, Wedgwood. Fifty years ago
I tried to crack that code of women's talk,
Thinking it would reveal to me the nine
Needs of women I would fulfill as a man.
What kind of fool would attempt to understand?

Ah, friend, you're homesick. I know the welling pain
That follows us from childhood's hearth to the grave.
What should we tell you to sweeten the memories
You took such trouble to pack and carry with you
This far, only to find them troubling your sleep?
You too will make a poetry of this pain,
Draw into your lines the power to change
The leaf, blossom, and bole of Yeats's trope
Into your own code for the heart's troubled seasons.

II Landscapes

Come down the steep trail to a place nearby
Where thermals eddy from the valley floor
Along the layers of the sandy cliff

Into the perfect turquoise bowl of sky.
Martins dive from their little caves
Into clouds of mosquitoes. Warm air rises
To hold the red-tail hawk aloft,
His head sidelong, spying on the rattler
Who spies on the fieldmouse slipping out
To sip from the edge of Hangman Creek.

The heron stoops gray from her gray log
Over the pool where the dappled trout
Is finning upstream through shadowy reeds.
Gold fennel will scatter its sedative tang
Around our heads when we start downstream
Through the tambourine racket of crickets,
So much in tune with the place we forget
This is not ours, this huge dome of sky,
This Midas sun. This could never be ours.

A few months more will steal our time.
Wind will blow down the leaves, then snow
Against the house, then Spring, too late
To grow a few bean-rows in time
To bear a crop before summer when we're due
Back on our island, the shock of landfall
After the long flight: the intense green
Under the rushing clouds, the small fields,
The hedges flecked with fuscia, the gossiping rooks.
The sharp essential odors of grass and sea.

Drink and talk with the family, you
With yours up North, and we, as usual,
Among the glasshouse pleasantries of ours

In the Republic. We'll tell of this hard place,
Its wonders, as if we wouldn't really mind
Returning here to live—although we know
Nothing could make this home. Nothing on earth.

Easter, Key Biscayne

for Irv Broughton

A broker in a linen suit was beaming
Piecharts onto a screen behind the dais,
Forecasting modest growth if goals, et cetera—
Tedium of conferences drove him
From the Columbus Room to ride the glass
Bubble up the hotel wall to his room
Over the marina's tilting masts
And clumsy pelicans. He changed.

Tan shorts, green polo shirt, sandals, a white
Hotel towel draped round his neck, he drove
The rented car to the beach and parked it where
He could hear the ocean behind a range of dunes.
He walked a trail through sawgrass and pine shade
Bordering some opulent villa's gardens.
Whiff of oleander, bougainvillea.

Flux of sunned bodies up and down the beach.
Tedium of uncertainty before he set off south
Along the tideline till he reached the bridge
That linked the keys to the mainland, then turned back
By the hedge that hid the pampered villa grounds.
Was this the disgraced president's retreat?
A druglord's? A corporate pirate's tax break?
He spread the stolen towel and stretched out.

He found himself, a nearly naked voyeur,
The object of such casual regard
As other sunclad worshippers could afford

For his alabaster torso, his flushed visage.
Filling his range of vision, the oiled flesh,
Stripped of personality, genitals
Covered by the merest dayglo lycra,
Paraded between him and the rippling edge

Of the ocean. Consider this ample blonde
In the orange string bikini, and her muscle-boy.
What could he know of her true being? What more
Than this concupiscent mirage? He rose,
Charged down the sand like a tilting knight, and plunged
Into milky star-studded water. He picked up
An easy overarm stroke, a slow roll

Through drifting, bubbling space beyond the range
Of any signal except his own breath leaving
A sparkling trail in the creamy interim
Between beach and empty sky. He dolphined down
As far as the lifeguard's chair and back to wade
Up through lengthening shade, where brown couples
Lounged like Gauguin's islanders in the perfumed heat,
Accepting all that was, its mystery.

Discharge

from *Hospital*

Her voice is an octave above
the unbearable disinfectant
THIS EXPLAINS WHAT TO DO she yells
right into my headache when you
get home BE SURE BE SURE BE SURE
four times a day with meals
don't lift your weight if you feel
or the other be sure to check
sign here where it says signature
so YOU PAY YOU PAY YOU PAY
or we take everything you have left
take all your things with your things
kidney-bowl eyewash pills
FOR PAIN FOR PAIN FOR PAIN
this is the wheelchair to go
the distance from room four oh six
to ground level be sure
not to walk till you can walk
out without suing us
TAKE CARE NOW

Self-Portrait, with Masks

Homage to Rembrandt

I

Another version of that serious boy
Tried on a frown, a leer, a cocked
Eyebrow, locked in the upstairs bathroom
With imaginary partners. He spoke
Sternly to them from the silent side
Of the brute who wrestled other brutes
In the playground to earn a tough-guy name
Losing more than he won in any game.

Was it Onan made him vain, pale?
Ah, that stone-faced town, where they still
Think every thought's a sin and every mirror
Stares at its sinner and the stout priest
Sets the price of absolution at a rate he knows
Can't be paid. This mask is hollow-cheeked,
Lit from inside like a Halloween lantern
Hanging in Hell's darkest cavern.

II

Look yourself in the eye
Though light and mirror be poor.
Take note of that stare. Take the whole
Face on its own terms, set
Like a fortress on the curve
Of shadowy shoulders—paint
Stroked and thumbed into place—
To what end? *Understand me*

(It speaks, this familiar mask),
Posterity is not my master.
Nor is blindfold fate. Nor am I
My own creator. Pray for me.

The Gingriad: An Aor

So swells each windpipe; ass intones to ass;

Harmonic twang! Of leather, horn, and brass;

—Pope

Prologue

He's pudding white, like a lab rat on meds,
He's a beady-eyed dealer in chicken mire.
See how he puckers to kiss the heads
Of those TV mikes? Will they sate his desire?
He's the Speaker of the House of Votes.
He can tell the weasels from the stoats.
He lectures often with the avid goodwill
Of a veteran bootlicker raising a shine
On the asses of rich folk who pay him to whine
About ignorant people who choose to be poor.
"If they work at whatever they're qualified for
The free market forces will fix everything."
His moonface smile's a pig's ass on a swing.
He knows about pigs, this hog-heaven hero,
With his hog-bristle hair and his jowls like Nero.

Pigtale One

Here's a bedtime story, children, about our sappy sage.
Once upon a time, he was given a pet,
A little brown pig in a little wire cage.

The Aor is a form from Irish Bardic poetry, defined in Dineen's Dictionary as "a lampoon, satire, or personal attack."

Yes! You guessed! A guinea-pig! Did he use it to test
His social theories? Too young for that yet?
Well, he fed and he fed his little house-guest,
Till the Newts moved house, so with no regrets
He gave another kid this very, VERY fat
BIG guinea-pig now, in a cage so small
That just moving around had rubbed away all
The pretty brown fur from his big pink rump,
And he couldn't move that ass-dragging hump.
—The guinea-pig I mean, not the Speaker of the Pack
Who rose from 'umble origins to be the crackerjack
Ideal of the fast-talking *Wunderkind*
Who delivers American History, plucked and skinned
On closed-circuit pay-TV, where the suckers are found—
And he can find them anywhere, thick on the ground.
You'd swear the way he talks he owns the very Red Delicious
With Adam's bite on it, which proves Eve was the vicious
Unwed Welfare Mother who causes all poo' chilluns
To be dependin' on the State and who causes all the killins.'
You sure he doesn't *have* that apple? You sure the ark on Ararat
Wasn't actually sabotaged by that guy Arafat?

Pigtale Two

Having had a vision as a direct consequence
Of consorting with consultants (whose well-developed sense
Of where the quick bucks can be made is making history),
This History Professor professes wistfully
His historic brand-new Vision for updating all Creation
To make it safe for the Christian rich and the polyester Nation.
All others, says our pundit, must get in line to feed
Below the trough if he would lead them when he gets to lead.

If they listen and take heed, they will certainly ascend
To Orwellian Olympias so scrupulously planned
That every camp for orphans will have its marching band,
And every little fascist have Big Brother for a friend.

Meanwhile murky Murdoch, the paper plutocrat,
Who among the fat rats is the fattest of the fat,
Reasons with Herr Sprecher, "Put money in thy purse, Sir!"
A twist in the plot, you think? It gets worser and worser!
With Murdoch's mighty millions, he's going to mix some muck,
Then stick it all together in a big fat book!
But soon the muck turns into dust, and his greedy gamble
Blows off in front of everyone and makes a TV shambles!
He smirks and smiles, he shucks and jives, he knows we think it funny
That his book is getting published, but he doesn't get the money!

Pigtale Three

His ungulate smile is slick as slime.
He's not so easily chastened.
He flurries forth—*Election time!*
He hollers loud, for time's a-wastin'!
Welfare fraud! Drugs and Crime!
Pork for me and my Party!
He's for Future Schlock
And high-yield stock
And that's just for a start. He
Has plans to do more for the poor.
He'll cut them off
From the public trough
And they'll just disappear.

But that's not his creepiest concoction.
This Master of Bamboozle goes into action.
First he assembles his Key Advisors
(A score or two of wealthy old misers)
In a swishy Nevada resort.
There in the sun he'll extort
Every dollar he can from these hogs
Who feel lucky as old sun-gods
That it's he who's getting their cash
For GOPAC, his personal stash—
A cool hundred million to pay
For oiling, the oldfashioned way,
The party machine. It's all spent,
Down to the last greasy cent,
On campaigns of slander and smear
That make all but fanatics keep clear
Of the voting booths. All this is *legal!*
Could God's anointed do evil?

Then he goes around TV-land telling
How badly his enemy's smelling.
He tells the lie, repeats the lie, goes back on television
To give the lie to telling lies by way of repetition.
"The poor don't vote, they've no ambition,
"So they're to blame for their condition.
"The bankers hate public health insurance, so
"We'll let the wealthy sickies keep their dough.
"You know, if you-all got to know all we know
About the opposition, you'd be sick."
There's no real muck that he can get to stick
But nothing can stop this pig from winging it
When the Murdoch gang is slinging it.

Fewer than half the voters show up for the election.
This means a landslide for the Porcine Connection.
Everyone's gagging on the stench off the pond
And most keep their distance, but the Gadarene are fond
Of the stink around Congress. They gladly take over
And wallow with cute Newt in the well-manured clover.
Gets caught with three hundred grand in bribes. Pleads remorse.
Gets up and whimpers. Gets off. He needs a Curse:

Newt Goes to Pigneywood!

Stroke your little mikehead. Go on, simper and pucker.
Okay, enough already, you lardfaced mikesucker.
We interrupt your program with this click on the Cursor,
So superior to the fan as a rapid-fire shit-disperser.
Your Contract on America, your trickle-down hickory-dickory,
Has no more chance, for all your sickly trickery,
Than a snowball where you're going. Your presence is requested
In the Leather-Horn-and-Brass Room where your mettle will be
        tested
By the good ole boys from Bob Jones U.
And the jack-off team at the *Natty Review*
And the recycled wits of the Heritage Center.
Madam Helmsley has most graciously lent her
Talent and thongs to ride you round the orgy
In your little rubber jockstrap—ole Porgy from Georgy!
She'll lead you by that ring in your cute li'l piggy nose
And prod you in the withers with her big hunk of hose.
You'll be on the Disney Channel as Eternity progresses
Dressed up fine and dandy in feathers and molasses.
Then matrons with huge bosoms will come to steam you clean—
You'll have lots of kinky fun with *their* guinea-pig routine!

You mean you're not enjoying this? You feel you're a *victim?*
Dick Nixon's down there, talk to him—he *loves* them to afflict him!
He'll take you round to play with all the most unfeeling fascists
Who'll crunch your crotch and scratch your eyes and light your farts
      with matches.
Then by dawn's early light they'll give you the *coup de grâce*—
The Stars and Stripes forever, on a flagpole, up your ass.